Michael Faraday

by MARY BETH SPANN

With the Editors of TIME FOR KIDS

Table of Contents

CHAPTER 1
A SCIENTIST'S BEGINNINGS

An Unlikely Scientist

Michael Faraday was the last person you would have expected to become a great **scientist**. He was born poor. He had very little schooling. But his discoveries about electricity changed the world!

Michael Faraday as a young man

Faraday was born near London, England, on September 22, 1791. His father, a blacksmith, was often sick and not able to work. Faraday remembered times when his family had just one loaf of bread to last the whole week.

As a child, Faraday learned how to read, write, and work with numbers. He loved to read. Later in life, he said it was reading that had allowed him to teach himself science. Once he had taught himself science, he was on his way to becoming a great scientist.

London in the early 1800s

Birth of a Bookworm

When he was about fourteen, Faraday left school. He needed to help earn money for his family. Faraday became an apprentice to George Reibau. Reibau was a well-known bookbinder.

Reibau taught Faraday how to take printed pages and bind them together inside covers. In his free time, Faraday read many of the books on which he worked. He liked the encyclopedia and science books best. A family friend described him as "the best bookworm for eating his way to the inside [of books]!"

Reibau encouraged Faraday to study science. He gave him the time and space to do experiments with **static electricity**.

A nineteenth-century bookbinder at work

Reibau also urged Faraday to take notes about everything he read. Note-taking was something Faraday did for the rest of his life. Today, scientists still read the notes Faraday made.

Faraday was influenced by a book called *Conversations in Chemistry* by Jane Marcet. The book about **chemistry** had been written for young people. It was easy to understand. Faraday said Marcet's book gave him "a foundation in this science."

The book also taught Faraday how to explain scientific ideas simply and clearly. Years later, people who were not scientists said they understood Faraday's ideas because he explained them so well.

Faraday in Focus

Faraday later described how his reading had changed him: "I could believe in…[fairy tales] as easily as in the Encyclopedia. But facts were important and saved me. I could trust a fact."

Shocking!

Have you ever petted a cat's fur and heard crackling sounds? Or walked on a carpet and then felt a shock when you touched a doorknob? This happens because small energy particles, called **electrons**, "jump" from one surface to another. This is a form of electricity called static electricity.

Faraday Speaks Out

Faraday wanted to begin teaching other people about science. He wanted to speak to audiences. To learn to speak well, he asked a friend to help him improve his grammar. He studied grammar two hours a week for seven years! Faraday was able to improve as a scientist because he asked for help with learning.

In 1810, at the age of 19, Faraday joined a club to talk about all kinds of ideas. The club members helped him think about and explore different ideas in science. It was at a club meeting that Faraday gave his first speeches about science.

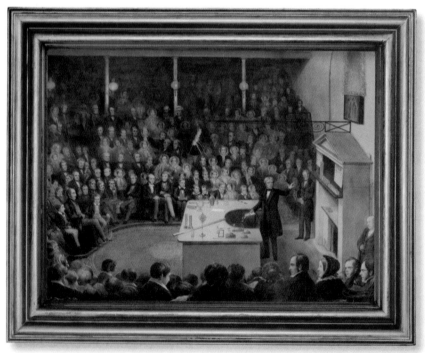

Faraday speaks to the general public about science.

Meeting an Important Chemist

In 1812, Faraday was given a ticket to attend some talks about chemistry. The speaker was Sir Humphrey Davy. Davy was an important chemist. Faraday enjoyed Davy's talks so much that he decided to work with him. Since he had learned bookbinding, Faraday bound his own notes

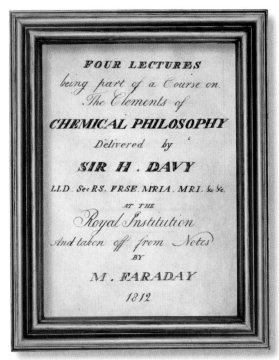

into a book about Davy's lectures. He sent the book and a letter to Davy. In the letter, Faraday asked for work. At first, there were no job openings. But soon after, Davy offered Faraday a job as his assistant.

Ideas at Work!

A **theory** is an idea that helps explain things. Scientists have theories about the way things work, change, move, live, or grow. Scientists test their theories with science experiments. They explain their theories to other scientists. These tests and explanations help show whether a theory makes sense.

CHAPTER 2
NEW DISCOVERIES AHEAD

Time for Travel

Faraday jumped at the chance to work with Davy. Together, they traveled to France and other places in Europe. But a war was going on in Europe at the time. Davy and Faraday had to get permission to travel from the ruler of France. That ruler was the famous Napoleon Bonaparte!

Davy and Faraday used this instrument in their experiments with light.

In Europe, Faraday took part in Davy's research in chemistry.

Faraday in Focus

Faraday kept a journal of his travels with Davy. By the time he returned home, he had written 400 pages about their adventures and discoveries.

In one experiment in Italy, Davy and Faraday set fire to a diamond. They heated the diamond with rays from the Sun. They had set up the experiment so that the Sun's rays passed through two giant-sized lenses.

By the time Faraday had finished working with Davy, he knew as much about chemistry as anyone in the world.

What Is Chemistry?

Do you spend time inside buildings? Do you ride in cars? Do you buy clothes? Do you eat food from the supermarket? If you answered "yes" to any of those questions, you can thank the science of chemistry.

Chemistry supplies the materials used in making buildings, cars, clothes and food. Chemistry is the study of elements and how they join together.

Elements are metals and nonmetals that cannot be broken down. Metals are solids. They have a definite shape and take up a definite amount of space. They can conduct (or carry) electricity. Iron, copper, and zinc are three important elements that are metals. Nonmetals (except carbon) do not conduct electricity. Hydrogen and oxygen are nonmetal elements.

Today, more than 110 elements have been identified. Scientists are discovering more elements all the time. Most can be combined with other elements. They can form new substances called **compounds**. Some compounds are found in nature. Water is a natural compound of hydrogen and oxygen. Other compounds are made by scientists.

This is the chemical set Michael Faraday used in his experiments.

On to Electricity

In 1820, Michael Faraday became curious about the work of Hans Christian Oersted. Oersted had discovered the link between **electricity** and **magnetism**. He proved that when electricity was passed through a wire, and the wire was close to a magnetic needle in a compass, the needle moved.

This diagram shows one of Faraday's experiments with electromagnetism.

Electromagnets are made when wire is coiled around a magnetic core material, such as iron. When an **electric current** passes through the coiled wire, the core material becomes magnetized.

Faraday went further than Oersted. In 1821, he invented the first electric motor! Yet in spite of his interest in electricity and magnetism, Faraday spent the next ten years speaking to audiences about science.

Modern electric motors are based on Faraday's discoveries.

Days of Discovery

In 1831, Faraday decided to focus again on the study of electricity and magnetism. In just ten days, he discovered that a magnetic field could be used to control an electric current flowing through a wire. This meant that electricity could be used to run machines. The electric current could be moved back and forth or turned on and off. Today, **technology** based on Faraday's discovery is used in many machines, such as trains and microphones.

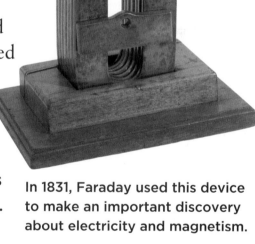

In 1831, Faraday used this device to make an important discovery about electricity and magnetism.

Faraday in Focus

Faraday helped come up with the words *electrode*, *electrolyte*, *anode*, *cathode*, and *ion*. Use a dictionary to find out what these words mean.

CHAPTER 3
A GIFT TO SCIENCE

A Brighter Light

In 1836, Faraday was made Scientific Advisor to Trinity House. Trinity House was (and still is) in charge of safe boating around the shores of England and Wales. Lighthouses at that time used

big oil-burning lamps to guide boats and ships. Faraday decided the oil-burning chimneys in these lighthouses could be made better.

In the early 1840s, Faraday invented a chimney

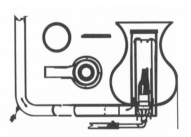

A drawing of Faraday's design for an oil-burning chimney

for burning oil in a better way. The invention was placed in lighthouses and in important buildings, such as Buckingham Palace. This is the home of the British Royal family.

Final Years

In the early 1840s, Faraday's health began to fail. Even so, he continued to carry out science experiments. He discovered that a magnetic force could change light. He did this by placing a piece of heavy glass on the poles of a powerful electromagnet. Then he passed light through the glass. When he turned on the electromagnet, he saw that the state of light had changed. Later, he tried the same experiment by hanging the glass. This time, the glass moved. That told Faraday that the light and the glass had both been affected by the magnetic force. He drew the conclusion that a magnetic force was present in all matter. This discovery was called the Faraday Effect.

Michael Faraday's discoveries helped make many forms of modern communication possible.

The Write Stuff

Michael Faraday died on August 25, 1867. He left behind about 4,800 notes and letters. They had been written throughout his life. His notes tell the story of his bookbinding days, his days as a speaker, and his experiments. His letters went to scientists and political leaders around the world.

A page from Michael Faraday's journal

Faraday's writings let us look into the mind of this great scientist. We do not have to guess about his thoughts or experiments. People read his writings today to learn firsthand about his love for science and his many discoveries.

Write It Down!

Here's how to keep a notebook or journal like Michael Faraday's!

- Write every day. Date your entries.
- Use plain language and write in ink.
- Number the pages as you go along.
- Write what you have learned each day and how you have learned it.
- Begin each day's entry on a new page.
- Include drawings, if you like.
- Review your entries to see how much you have learned!

Glossary

chemistry (KEM-uh-stree) the science that deals with the nature of substances (page 5)

compound (KOM-pownd) two or more elements joined together *(page 9)*

electric current (i-LEK-trik KUR-uhnt) the flow of an electrical charge *(page 10)*

electricity (i-lek-TRIS-i-tee) energy made by the flow of electrons *(page 10)*

electron (i-LEK-tron) a particle outside the nucleus (center) of an atom *(page 5)*

magnetism (MAG-ni-tiz-uhm) a force that attracts iron, steel, or other metals *(page 10)*

scientist (SIGH-uhn-tist) a person who studies living things or the world by measuring, testing, and experimenting *(page 2)*

static electricity (STAT-ik i-lek-TRIS-i-tee) the buildup of an electrical charge on a material *(page 4)*

technology (tek-NOL-uh-jee) use of science for practical purposes *(page 11)*

theory (THEE-uh-ree) ideas that explain something but need to be proved *(page 7)*

Index